Celebration Puzzle Pieces

WORSHIP NOTEBOOK 2 FOR KIDS

The Church Year

Judith A. Christian

Illustrated by Jim Siegfried

CPH
Concordia Publishing House

*Thanks to David Christian for his contributions to the manuscript,
and to Jane Haas for her careful reading of early drafts.*

*Special thanks to former students at Christ Community,
Kirkwood, Missouri, and to Jolene Vogel
who brought special meaning and exuberance to celebration.
I'll always remember!*

Scripture quotations taken from the HOLY BIBLE, NEW INTERNATIONAL VERSION®. NIV®. Copyright © 1973, 1978, 1984 by International Bible Society. Used by permission of Zondervan Publishing House. All rights reserved.

Text copyright © 2000 Judith A. Christian

Illustrations copyright © 2000 Concordia Publishing House

Published by Concordia Publishing House
3558 S. Jefferson Avenue, St. Louis, MO 63118-3968
Manufactured in the United States of America

1   2   3   4   5   6   7   8   9   10   09 08 07 06 05 04 03 02 01 00

Contents

First Things First

Using This Book

Welcome to *Celebration Puzzle Pieces!* Your interest in leading children toward a greater understanding of worship has led you to open these pages. You might be a pastor, professional educator, youth leader, volunteer teacher, or parent. Whatever your role, this book is designed for you!

It is called a *Worship Notebook* because it has been written in the format of an activity book. The pages can be reproduced and compiled into a folder or notebook. Some activities require pencil and paper, while others require imagination and interaction. They can be read aloud and serve as a springboard for further discussion, taught as part of a lesson or absorbed silently.

The possibilities are endless! Adapt this book according to your needs. Remember that adults will also benefit through the **TakeNoteTogether** pages. Send them home along with your own words of encouragement as part of God's family of faith!

Judith A. Christian

For Kids!

Y ou are not alone in your faith. At your Baptism, God brought you into His family, a special community—a "Christ community." We call this community "the Church." By the power of the Holy Spirit, you will grow and learn in this community throughout your life.

Every year there are gathering times when you remember and celebrate the events that are important to your family (birthdays and anniversaries, for example). It is important to the members of your family that you are a part of these times. Their presence and participation are important to you too. As you join in these celebrations, you come to know more about your family and your care for the family grows.

The *church year* provides celebrations that help you know more about Jesus and grow in your love for Him and for His community—the Church. God wants you to join His family of faith in these celebrations. And His family—the Church—needs you and your special gifts as it gathers to hear and to share God's saving action for all people.

God will bless you as you celebrate in the name of Jesus!

For Grown-Ups:
TakeNoteTogether!

Every worship is a festival—a little Easter—when we remember the life, death, and resurrection of our Savior, Jesus Christ.

Much like a puzzle, each festival in the church year is necessary so that the entire picture of the story of salvation can be clearly seen. Communicating the mighty acts of God (the puzzle pieces) from one generation to the next, from parent to child, is a precious gift you can give to your child.

Remembering and rehearsing God's mighty acts, helps children and adults grow together in their understanding of faith and their commitment to Jesus. It helps them see themselves as a significant part of the story—an important and much-needed piece of the puzzle. The more focused we remain on the story of salvation in Jesus, the more memorable the festivals are likely to be for our children.

Most festivals in the church year celebrate the life of Jesus and our growth in faith. *Celebration Puzzle Pieces* focuses on those celebrations. Some church celebrations relate to milestones in the life of a specific congregation, denomination, or institution. While those times are also important, they have not been included in this book.

May your participation in the celebrations of the Church—God's family of faith—be a blessing to you, your children, and your congregation.

God's Family

Family of Faith

"Go home to your family and tell them how much the Lord has done for you, and how He has had mercy on you" (Mark 5:19).

The name of my family of faith is:

_____

(Write the name of your church.)

The place where my family of faith gathers to celebrate looks like this:

Add a photo or draw a picture of the church where you worship.

> Church is a special place
> to be with God,
>   to talk with God,
>   to listen to God, and
> to hear the stories of God.

Puzzle Pieces

Church Year

There is a time for everything, and a season for every activity under heaven (Ecclesiastes 3:1).

Each year the family of faith hears the story of the mighty acts God has done to save His people. The story has many parts. Each part is a festival, a time when the church remembers and celebrates what God has done and what He is still doing.

You know that every piece is needed to make a jigsaw puzzle complete. Each piece of the story about your loving, powerful God is important too. Each of the Church's celebrations (festivals) is like a piece of a puzzle with a special theme and color. Read about the colors of the church year.

BLUE, the color of hope, is often used during Advent when the family of faith waits for the coming of the Lord.

WHITE is the color of holiness and the glory of God. It is used for Christmas, Epiphany, and Easter because these are the days we celebrate the glory of our holy Lord.

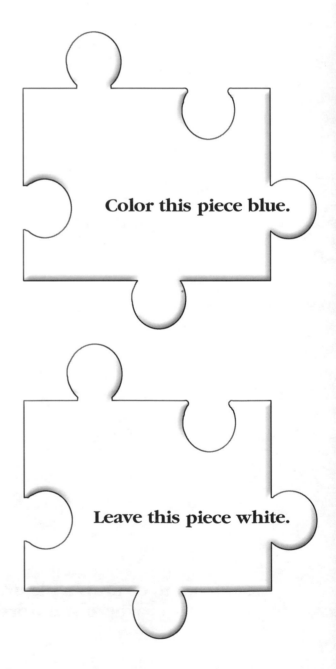

Color this piece blue.

Leave this piece white.

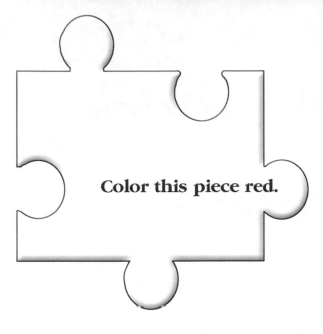

Color this piece red.

RED is the color of fire and blood. It is used for times we celebrate the Holy Spirit and His work or when we remember the life and death of people who died for Jesus.

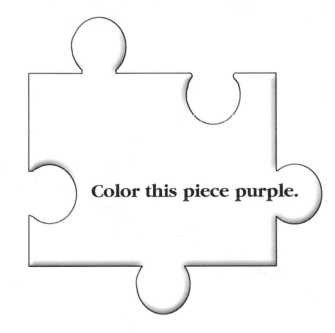

Color this piece purple.

PURPLE is mainly used at times when we feel sorry, especially about the wrong things we do—our sins. It is used during the season of Lent and sometimes during Advent.

Outline this piece with black.

BLACK is used for times of sadness in worship such as death or grief and it is used on Good Friday. Black is a deep, serious color.

Color this piece green.

GREEN is the color of life and growth, especially the new life we have in Jesus. Green is used during the seasons of Epiphany and Pentecost.

LOOK FOR THE COLORS IN YOUR CHURCH.

WATCH TO SEE WHEN THE COLORS CHANGE.

Puzzle Pieces

God's Story

God's story is also *your* story. All of God's actions are done for *you*. Jesus was sent to live, die, and rise for you. You are needed as an important piece of the puzzle in God's story. **Create *your* piece of the puzzle by drawing a picture of yourself.**

TakeNoteTogether

Enriching Activities for Kids and Their Grown-Ups

Puzzle Pieces

Church Year

Family traditions developed around the church year can build lasting bridges between the Christian home and the Church. Festivals of the church year give us the opportunity to look both forward and backward. As we pack away celebration decorations, we reflect on the past and wonder about the future.

Celebrations require leadership and participation. In a family, a grown-up takes the role of leader and involves other members in planning and preparation. The involvement of each family member is essential if the experience is to be meaningful for everyone.

Religious and folk traditions are valuable sources from which to draw when planning a celebration.

 Begin now to establish traditions that are taken from the past, adapted to the present, and will propel you into the future.

 Determine what occasions you will celebrate, with whom, where, and how you will make them special and memorable.

 Assign each member of the family (include toddlers and preschool children!) a specific task and help one another fulfill responsibilities.

 Keep focused on the true reason for the festival—Jesus. Ask God to bring your family closer to Jesus through your celebration.

 Plan worship as a meaningful part of every family celebration. Thank God for His goodness and for the special gifts each family member brings to the celebration.

11

Sundays

Sabbath

God blessed the seventh day and made it holy, because on it He rested from all the work of creating that He had done (Genesis 2:3).

Christians, people who believe in Jesus, have set aside a day of rest *(Sabbath)*, usually Sunday. This special day is a time for you and your faith family to:

* GATHER to worship,

* REMEMBER that God rested after His work of creating and

* CELEBRATE the new life God gives you through the resurrection of His Son, Jesus.

Make Sundays extra special by praying a blessing for each person in your family. Write the name of each family member in a "blessing shape" below. Read the examples, then write your own words of blessing for each one. Every Sunday, pray each blessing—beginning with the oldest person in your family.

_____ may God help you do your work this week.

_____ may God keep you safe when you play.

_____

_____

_____

TakeNoteTogether

Enriching Activities for Kids and Their Grown-Ups

Sundays

Sabbath

It is important to set aside a day of rest *(Sabbath)*. It is even more important to set aside special time for worship. Make Sundays a time of worship and a time for family.

For Church:

* Plan to attend and participate in worship.

* Build anticipation by predicting what may happen in worship.

* Read in advance the prescribed Scripture readings for worship. (Contact your church office for the list of readings.)

* Sing or play songs or hymns that may be sung.

* Set out special clothes the night before.

For Home:

* Have special things to eat.

* Go on a family outing.

* Prepare a special meal with a decorated table.

* Plan special activities; invite friends over.

* Bring out toys, play games, or read books that have been reserved for Sunday.

* Pray a blessing for each family member, beginning with the oldest.

Having time to be a family is vital!

Note: Be sure each family member has a turn to choose favorite foods, activities, outings, etc.

13

PART 1:
The Time of
CHRISTMAS

The birth of Jesus is the *main event*.

We prepare for this event during the four weeks of **Advent**.

We celebrate the event during the twelve days of **Christmas**.

We learn what the event means for us during the weeks after **Epiphany**.

The Season of
ADVENT

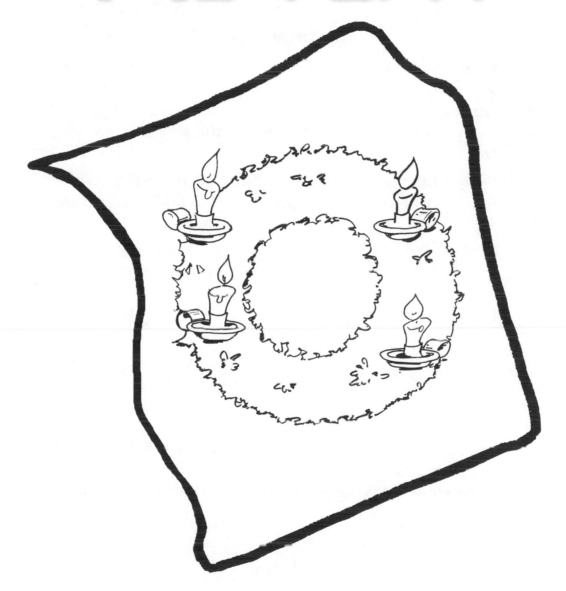

The Four Weeks before Christmas

Color: Blue

Waiting

Advent

Rejoice greatly … see, your King comes to you (Zechariah 9:9).

Advent begins the church year. During Advent the family of God *waits* and *gets ready* to celebrate the birthday of Jesus. We hear the Bible stories about the angels who told Zechariah, Mary, and Joseph that God would send the promised Savior as a baby.

People long ago waited many, many years for the coming of Jesus. We wait the four weeks of Advent and pray, "Come, Lord Jesus." Advent is the season of waiting.

Waiting is hard. Watch for the wonderful hints, tastes, and signs of Advent. Gather clues that tell you Jesus' birthday is coming.

Clip Advent words from worship service folders and glue them in this picture frame. What else can be added? Scraps of ribbon? Wrapping paper? Wait, watch, collect, and create!

Come, Lord Jesus. By _____

Waiting

Advent

Family traditions developed around the church year can build lasting bridges between a Christian home and the congregation. Here are some ideas for this season:

Make or buy an Advent wreath. The wreath, which consists of four candles standing in a ring of evergreen twigs, represents the coming of Christ into a dark world. The circle reminds us of God's never-ending love and the candles of the light of Christ. On each of the four Sundays in Advent, a new candle is lit, so that by the Sunday before Christmas all four candles are burning. A fifth white candle (often placed in the center of the wreath) is lit on Christmas Day.

Light a candle on each Sunday in Advent when the family is gathered. Say the following words as the candles are lit:

The candle lighter says: "Come, Lord Jesus."

  All others say: "And bring love." *(week 1)*;

      "And bring hope." *(week 2)*;

      "And bring peace." *(week 3)*;

      "And bring joy." *(week 4)*

When lighting the white Christmas candle,
the candle lighter says: "Jesus our Savior is born today."

  All others reply: "Glory to God in the highest.
      Peace to His people on earth."

Make an Advent calendar during the Thanksgiving weekend or just before the first Sunday of Advent. The Advent calendar helps to count the 25 days until Christmas morning. It can be as simple as 25 construction paper strips formed into a chain with interlocking loops. Remove one loop each day until all are gone.

The Season of
CHRISTMAS

December 25
Color: White

**Read the Christmas story in Luke 2:1–20
and Matthew 1:18–25.**

18

Happy Birthday!

The Nativity of Our Lord

Today in the town of David a Savior has been born to you; He is Christ the Lord (Luke 2:11).

The waiting is over. The joyful day is here! **Christmas** celebrates the birthday of God's gift to the world—His Son, Jesus.

Throughout the 12 days of Christmas (Christmas Day to the feast of the Epiphany) the story of the birth of Jesus unfolds. From the shepherds to the Wise Men, from Mary and Joseph to old Simeon and Anna, we hear that Jesus the child is also God, the promised Savior.

Another name for Jesus is Emmanuel, which means "God is with us." Young or old, small or big, rich or poor, Jesus is with all of His people. Jesus is with you.

You are an important part of His birthday celebration.

Pretend you baked a birthday cake for Jesus. How will you decorate it? What song will you sing for His birthday?

Christmas Wonder Walk

The Nativity of Our Lord

Plan a "Christmas Wonder Walk." Place creche figures (or other symbols of Christmas) throughout your home. Gather as a family and light a candle. The selected leader says: "The light of Christ." The family responds: "Thanks be to God."

The family moves to the first figure. The leader carries the lighted candle.

At each stop, family members read or tell a part of the Christmas story (Luke 2:1–20). (For example: Read Luke 2:1–3 at the starting point.) Then let a family member carry the figure as you continue to the next destination. Hold up the next figure then read verses 4–7, etc.

After each reading the leader says: "Glory to God in the highest." The family responds: "And peace to His people on earth."

Signal transitions with the ringing of a small bell or set of jingle bells. As you walk sing "O come let us adore Him, Christ the Lord." (Refrain from the carol "Oh, Come, All Ye Faithful," *Lutheran Worship*, Hymn 41).

Finally, stop at the Christmas tree and place the gathered objects on or under it. The candle is placed in a holder. The leader says: "The light of Christ." The family responds: "Thanks be to God."

Family members may receive a gift that reflects the birth of Christ (ornament, charm or other piece of jewelry, book, drawing, poem, or letter). Conclude with the singing of favorite Christmas songs or hymns.

Note: Consider saving some Christmas gifts to open on each of the 12 days of Christmas. This will extend the Christmas joy and delight. Mark some packages "Do not open until the third day of Christmas" or "Do not open until Epiphany."

The Season of
EPIPHANY

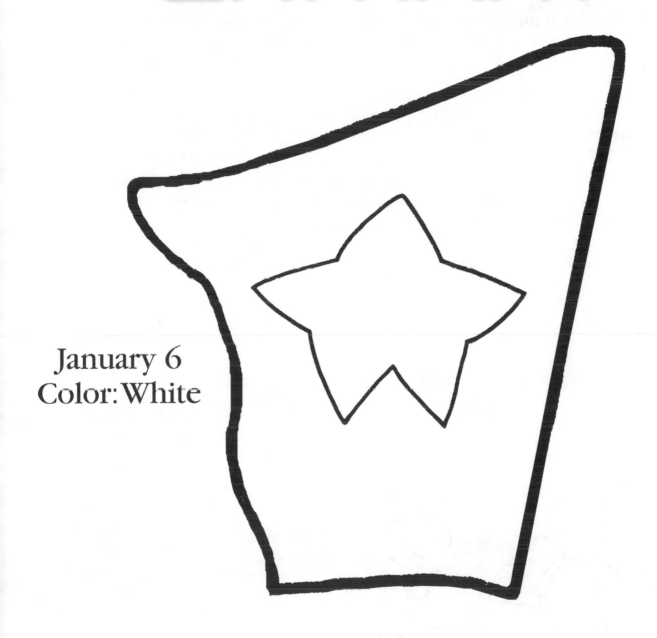

January 6
Color: White

Read the Epiphany story
in Matthew 2:1–12.

21

Star Bright

The Epiphany of Our Lord

We saw His star in the east and have come to worship Him (Matthew 2:2).

On the **Epiphany of our Lord** (January 6) we remember the visit of the Wise Men to Jesus. Following a bright star, they traveled a very long way to see Him.

The Wise Men are often called kings, but no one knows for certain if they really were. They brought very expensive gifts of gold, frankincense, and myrrh—gifts for a king. The visit of the Wise Men shows us that baby Jesus is the Ruler of our universe and the King born for all people.

Artists draw stars with different numbers of points to mean different things. A star drawn with five points is known as the Bethlehem star. It reminds us of the Wise Men whom God led to Jesus.

Pretend that you are studying the stars. Draw one that is different from all of the others.

Star Bright
The Epiphany of Our Lord

Epiphany is about gifts: those brought by the Wise Men, but more importantly God's gift of Jesus for all people. Throughout the Epiphany season we "unwrap" the gift of Jesus to better understand His glory.

Begin a tradition of putting the Christmas decorations away on January 6. Save a final gift for the family to open on this day.

Make and serve King Cake. Bake a favorite bundt cake with a small plastic figure of a baby (purchased at a craft store), a dried lima bean, or a jelly bean hidden inside. The person who discovers the hidden item is crowned king. The king then reads or tells the story of the visit of the Wise Men to Jesus. (Matthew 2:1–12).

Stars are important symbols this time of year. Stargaze on a clear night or visit a planetarium. As you look at the stars, use the Big Dipper to find the North Star. People have used that star to find their way at night for centuries because it doesn't move like the others. It reminds us of the light of Christ who always helps us find our way.

Plan a "Twelfth Night" party. Choose a day on a weekend near Epiphany. You may wish to invite 12 guests and give 12 small gifts. Decorate with a star theme. Serve King Cake.

Bless the family home. Here is one way:

* *If there is a family Advent wreath, begin and end the house blessing in the room where it is located.*

* *In each room, pray a brief prayer for the activities and people that occupy that space.*

* *Sing a stanza of a Christmas carol as you move from one space to another.*

* *Conclude with the Lord's Prayer or another prayer.*

The BAPTISM of Jesus

The First Sunday
after Epiphany

Color: White

**Read about Jesus' Baptism in Matthew 3:13–17,
Mark 1:9–11, and Luke 3:21–22.**

24

Marvelous!

The Baptism of Our Lord

"This is my Son, whom I love; with Him I am well pleased" (Matthew 3:17).

We celebrate the **Baptism of Jesus** on the first Sunday of Epiphany because it marks the beginning of Jesus' work telling others about God's love. Jesus went into the Jordan River to be baptized. As soon as HE stepped out of the water, heaven was opened and the Spirit of God came to HIM like a dove. Then a voice from heaven said, "This is my Son, whom I love ..."

That's marvelous!

At YOUR Baptism, the Spirit of God comes to YOU. This is the beginning of YOUR work. God has added YOU to His family to tell about the wonderful deeds of YOUR Savior, Jesus.

That's marvelous!

At YOUR Baptism the family of God welcomes YOU into the Lord's family and says, "We receive YOU as a fellow member of the body of Christ, a child of the same heavenly Father, to work with us in His kingdom." With these words and by the power of the Holy Spirit YOU became a church worker.

That's marvelous!

How many years, months, and days have YOU been a worker in God's kingdom? Count the years, months, and days from the day of YOUR Baptism until today and fill in the blanks.

> I have been a worker in God's kingdom for
>
> _____ years, _____ months, and _____ days.
>
> ## That's marvelous!

25

TakeNoteTogether

Enriching Activities for Kids and Their Grown-Ups

Simply Marvelous
The Baptism of Our Lord

Onward, Christian soldiers,
Marching as to war,
With the cross of Jesus going on before.

God calls each of us through Baptism to be a worker in His kingdom. Your family is on a mission for God.

 Find the baptismal certificates of each member of your household. (If you do not have one, your pastor or someone in the church office can help you get another one.) Frame the certificates and hang or display them so that you and the guests in your home are constantly reminded that workers in God's kingdom live in your house. Your baptismal certificates can also be reduced in size and laminated so that each family member can carry a copy of the certificate in a wallet or purse.

 Map out your mission. Ask yourselves:
* *Who do you know who needs to hear about Jesus and His kingdom?*
* *Who has wronged you or your family that needs to be forgiven?*
* *Who needs a helping hand or an act of kindness or a gift of love?*

 Evaluate your resources. What gifts has God distributed among the members of your household that He can use to bring forgiveness, healing, hope, and comfort to the situations you have identified?

 Do the work that God has, through your Baptism, called you to do. Marked by the Holy Spirit with the cross of Jesus, equipped with the Word of God and the Sacraments, and fortified by prayer, you are ready for God's mission—showing and telling others about His great love. You are workers in the kingdom of God, workers in His Church, and that is simply marvelous!

26

PART 2:
The Time of
EASTER

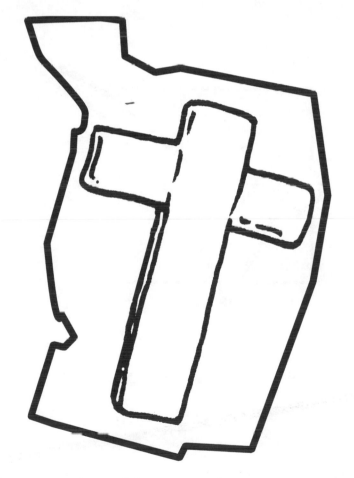

The death and resurrection of Jesus are the *main event*.

We prepare for the event during the **40 days of Lent**.

We celebrate the event on **Easter Day**.

We learn what the event means for us during the **seven weeks of Easter**.

The Season of LENT

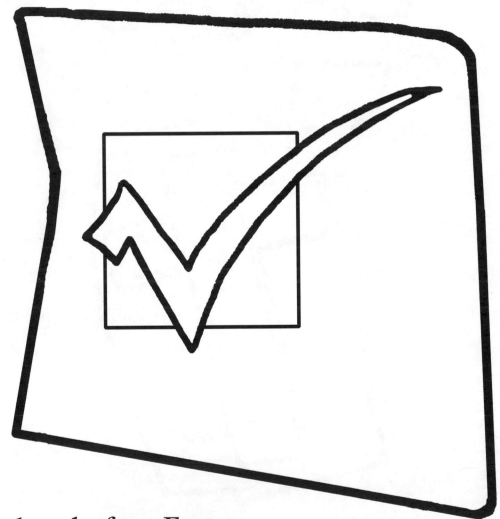

40 days before Easter,
(not including Sundays)

Color: Purple

28

Remembering

Days of Lent

Have mercy on me, O God, according to Your unfailing love (Psalm 51:1).

Lent is a time to remember your Baptism and your Christian work—telling others about Jesus. It is a quiet time for thinking about His suffering and death. The church puts "alleluia" away. The word is not sung or spoken during the season of Lent.

Lent lasts 40 days (not counting Sundays). The 40 days of Lent remind us of the 40 days Jesus spent in the desert before starting His work. Sometimes people give up something like eating candy or watching television during the season of Lent.

Lent is a time for remembering and telling the stories of the life of Jesus. You will get ready to celebrate Easter as you remember the mighty acts of God that save you from your sins and give you life forever with Him in heaven.

How will *you* get ready?

Memo

I can

I can

29

Remembering

Days of Lent

The name Lent comes from the old English word *lengten* that simply refers to the lengthening of days and the coming of spring. Lent lasts for 40 days. Forty is a symbolic number in the Bible. After 40 days and nights of rain and flood, Noah floated into a "new" world. God's chosen people entered the Promised Land after 40 years of journeying. Jesus fasted for 40 days in the wilderness. You can use the 40 days of Lent to reflect on your family's faith journey.

 Make a banner or poster with the words prayer, fasting, and giving. Together design symbols for each. Hang the banner in a prominent place to remind you to pray in new ways, to give something up, and to give out of thanks for what you have been given.

 Make mutual forgiveness a part of nightly prayers (be careful not to force forgiveness of one another until differences have been worked out). The language of forgiveness is "I forgive you because Jesus forgives me."

 Go for a Lenten walk or hike together. (Many churches view Lent as a time for a journey of faith.) Look for signs of "new life." Can you find buds on the branches? Where might animals be hibernating? Do you see very young animals or newly hatched birds?

 Plant seeds or bulbs together. Tulips, daffodils, and lilies have served as Easter symbols, partly because they grow from bulbs that look lifeless.

 Make pretzels together. Pretzels were first made in the fifth century as a Lenten bread (made with no dairy products, as was the custom during Lent). The traditional pretzel shape was intended to suggest prayer because at that time people crossed their arms over their chests when they prayed. Try crossing your arms like this when you pray during Lent.

Weeks before EASTER

6½ weeks
before Easter

Color:Purple

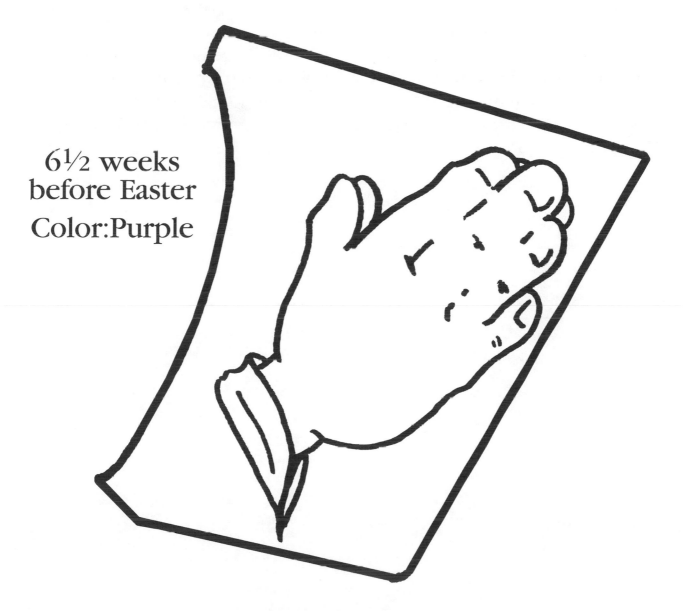

**You can read (and maybe memorize)
a Lenten call to repentance in Joel 2:12–13.**

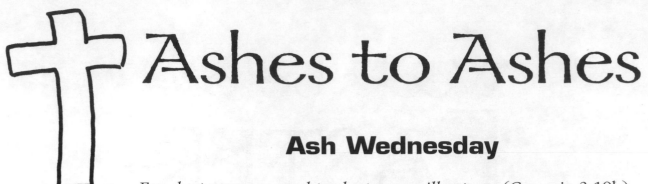 Ashes to Ashes

Ash Wednesday

For dust you are and to dust you will return (Genesis 3:19b).

Ash Wednesday is the first day of Lent. In some churches, ashes are used to draw a cross on the forehead of each member of the family of faith. Ashes are a reminder that sin wears you down to tiny bits and pieces (nothing). The death of Jesus on the cross and His resurrection put your bits and pieces back together. You are changed into someone special.

The sign of the cross is the holiest sign there is. It reminds you that by the love of Jesus you are marked and set apart as someone special who belongs to Him.

Fill this page with different signs of the cross.

Sixth Sunday in LENT

Sixth Sunday
in Lent

Color: Red

**Read the Palm Sunday story
in Matthew 21:1–11, Mark 11:1–10,
Luke 19:29–38, and John 12:12–15.**

33

Praise Parade

Palm Sunday

Hosanna to the Son of David! Blessed is He who comes in the name of the Lord! Hosanna in the highest! (Matthew 21:9).

On **Palm Sunday**, the family of faith tells about the time Jesus rode into the city of Jerusalem on a donkey. People were so excited to see Jesus coming that they cut down palm branches to wave and to throw down before Him.

In those days a king who came to fight in battle rode a horse. By riding into Jerusalem on a donkey, Jesus was telling everyone that He was a King coming in peace.

The crowds gathered and shouted, "Hosanna to the Son of David" and "Blessed is He who comes in the name of the Lord." They believed that He was the Messiah for whom they had been waiting. The church leaders got angry and told Jesus to stop the people from shouting. Jesus told them that if the people did not shout, stones would cry out instead.

Repeat the words the crowds shouted:

"Hosanna to the Son of David!
Blessed is He who comes in the name of the Lord!"

Join your faith family in singing or saying these words the next time you hear them in church.

Draw excited faces on these people in your faith family.

Pretend you are a newspaper reporter. Check your news source (Luke 19:28–48). Write the news stories for the *Jerusalem Times*. Draw your own "photos."

Jesus in Jerusalem!

"King" Comes to City
Crowds Disturb the Peace

Church Leaders Angered
Trouble in the Temple

HOLY WEEK

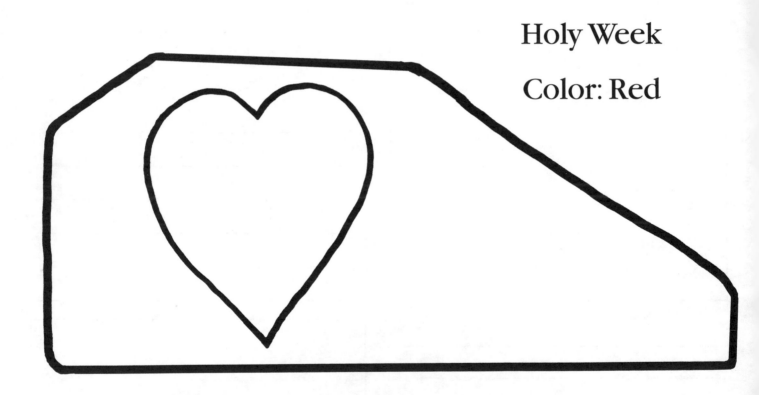

Holy Week

Color: Red

Read the foot-washing story in John 13:1–17. Read about Jesus' Last Supper with His disciples in Matthew 26:17–30, Mark 14:12–26, and Luke 22:7–23.

More Than Clean Feet

Maundy Thursday

Love one another. As I have loved you, so you must love one another (John 13:34).

Maundy Thursday celebrates a great feast of love. Jesus ate His last supper with His disciples, sharing with them His body and blood through the bread and wine, washing their feet, and commanding them to love one another.

Maundy Thursday brings you to the beginning of Jesus' suffering. Think of Jesus praying alone in the Garden of Gethsemane, knowing that the time of His death was near. Jesus' love for you is simple but awesome.

Jesus washed feet as a sign of His love. Think about how you can love and serve others as Jesus commands. This kind of love is not always easy. Remember Jesus washed the feet of *all* the disciples—even His betrayer, Judas.

What simple things can you do as a sign of Jesus' love? Finish the signs above to show your love actions.

More Than Clean Feet

Maundy Thursday

Every mealtime reminds us of Jesus' Last Supper.

 Make mealtime special. Decorate the table, light candles, use napkins (the designated color of the season of the church year), plan special treats or table favors. Practice mealtime etiquette. Invite Jesus to be your guest and remind one another of His loving presence at your table.

 Try interacting with words and actions that reflect forgiveness, service, and love. The family mealtime is essential to the life of the family and warrants time together and genuine, caring interaction. The time spent in family community is about more than sharing food. If regular mealtimes are a problem, plan one meal a week on a day when every family member can be present. (Begin positively by serving food everyone enjoys.)

 Plan ahead for everyone to participate in preparation, serving, and cleanup.

 Begin and end meals with prayer. Use different prayer forms. Read from the book of Psalms or learn and pray the words of a hymn. Read favorite Scripture passages for discussion and then pray about the things you discussed.

GOOD FRIDAY

Friday before Easter
Color: Black

Read about the crucifixion and death of Jesus in Matthew 27:32–56, Mark 15:21–41, Luke 23:26–49, and John 19:16–37.

39

God's Day

Good Friday

Jesus said, "It is finished." With that, He bowed His head and gave up His spirit (John 19:30).

Long ago **Good Friday** was called "God's Day" to remind His people that Jesus, who is God, died for them. The family of faith goes to church on Good Friday to remember the hour of Jesus' death. The church is dark and bare. Flowers and other decorations have been put away. Crosses may be covered with black cloth. Everything is quiet as God's people wait in sadness for the joy of Easter day.

You may wonder why the saddest day of the church year is called Good Friday. The day is truly a very sad day because you remember Jesus' death. It is also a happy day because it is the suffering and death of Jesus that takes away your sins.

Make the sign of the cross. Do it S-L-O-W-L-Y from forehead to chest and from left shoulder to right shoulder. Making the sign of the cross in this way, covers the whole you.

Jesus loves the *whole you*, so much that He stretched out His arms on a cross and died for you. Jesus loves the *whole you*, so much that He wants you to live with Him in heaven forever.

That's good.

HOLY SATURDAY

Saturday before Easter
Color: White

You can read about the burial of Jesus
in Matthew 28:57–66, Mark 15:42–47,
Luke 23:50–56, and John 19:38–42.

Getting Ready

Holy Saturday

So they went and made the tomb secure by putting a seal on the stone and posting the guard (Matthew 27:66).

Get ready for the most amazing miracle. Cover the wooden cross with flowers.

The day before Easter is called **Holy Saturday**. It is a day of waiting and getting ready. Something wonderful is going to happen, but you've got to wait. Are you ready?

Some churches use this day of waiting to celebrate the **Easter Vigil**. The faith family remembers God's great love for His people from the time of Adam and Eve until the time of YOU. This remembering sometimes takes a very long time—hours, in fact. But many think this day of vigil (waiting and getting ready) is the best part of Easter.

On Holy Saturday the family of faith gets ready to celebrate the most amazing miracle the world has ever seen—the resurrection of Jesus from the dead! Sometimes they get ready by decorating the church with lots and lots of flowers. How do you get ready?

Are you ready?

The Season of
EASTER

The first Sunday after the full moon
on or after March 21

Color: White

You can read about the empty tomb
in Matthew 28:1–8, Mark 16:1–8,
Luke 24:1–10, and John 20:1–9.

Jesus Is Alive!

The Resurrection of Our Lord

You are looking for Jesus ... Who was crucified. He has risen!
He is not here (Mark 16:6).

Alleluia! Easter is the most exciting day of the year. Jesus has burst out of the tomb and is alive forever!

Alleluia! Easter is the joyful celebration of the resurrection of Jesus.

Alleluia! The stories of Jesus are shared that let you know for sure that Jesus has died. Jesus is alive! Jesus will come again!

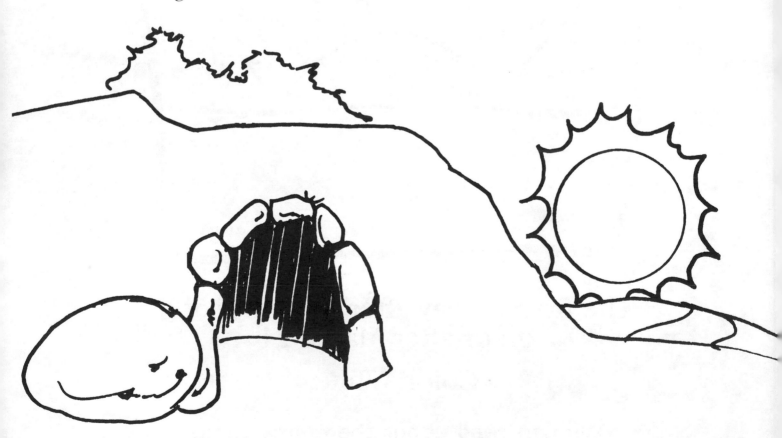

Pretend you are guarding the tomb where Jesus was buried. Draw what you see on Easter morning.

TakeNoteTogether
Enriching Activities for Kids and Their Grown-Ups

Jesus Is Alive!
The Resurrection of Our Lord

Easter day can be the most exciting and inspiring day of the year.

 First thing in the morning, gather the family and light a single large candle. As the candle is lit, the leader says, "The light of Christ." All others respond: "Alleluia! Christ is risen!"

 Having prepared 40 days for the coming of Easter, it is indeed a day to celebrate. One fairly universal tradition is the giving of Easter eggs. Decorate and give eggs to someone outside your family. Share the Easter news!

 People through the ages have responded to God's gift of forgiveness and new life at Easter by giving to those in need. Consult with family members and select a way you can respond.

 Watch a sunrise or attend an Easter sunrise service together. (If it's going to be cold, bring plenty of blankets.)

 Go for an Emmaus walk. This is an Easter Sunday or Monday tradition in much of Europe, but you can do it any time during the Easter season. Walk in the country or in a park and end with a picnic. Read or tell the story of the two people who met Jesus as they walked on the road to Emmaus (Luke 24:13–35).

The ASCENSION of Our Lord

Thursday, 40 days after Easter

Color: White

St. Luke tells the story of Jesus' ascension in Luke 24:50–53 and in Acts 1:1–11.

Up, Up, and Away

Ascension Day

He was taken up before their very eyes, and a cloud hid Him from their sight (Acts 1:9).

Jesus' return to His Father in heaven is celebrated on **Ascension Day**. Jesus is lifted up, up, and away into a cloud. He returns to the heavens. Before Jesus disappears into the clouds, He promises to send the Holy Spirit so that His work will be known in the hearts and actions of all who believe, including you.

During the 40 days from Easter to Ascension we remember how Jesus surprised His disciples in many places.

At first, the life, death, and resurrection of Jesus did not make sense to the disciples. It is not until Jesus leaves the earth and the power of the Spirit comes upon them that they finally "get it." Then they understand what Jesus really did in His days on earth. Now Jesus' work is to be their work. The words and actions of Jesus are to be their words and actions.

In the nine days between Ascension and Pentecost pray these words with your family of faith: "Come, Holy Spirit!"

Do you "get it?"

Imagine that you are one of the disciples watching Jesus rise to heaven. Draw what you see. Do you wonder what the disciples were thinking and feeling?

47

PENTECOST

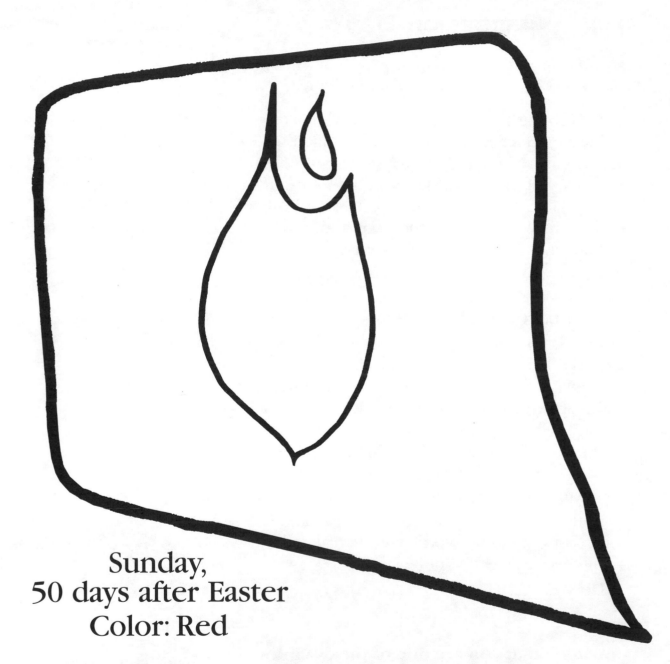

Sunday,
50 days after Easter
Color: Red

**You can read the story of Pentecost
in Acts 2:1–21.**

48

Got the Spirit!

Pentecost

All of them were filled with the Holy Spirit and began to speak in other tongues as the Spirit enabled them (Acts 2:4).

Pentecost is celebrated as the birthday of the Christian Church. It is the day that people took over the work Jesus had begun. Pentecost is one of the great festivals of the church year. The family of faith celebrates the coming of the Holy Spirit.

On the first Pentecost, the disciples of Jesus sat in a room waiting for the Holy Spirit who had been promised by Jesus when He returned to heaven. They heard the Spirit come as a mighty wind and saw tiny flames above their heads. The Holy Spirit filled the hearts of the disciples. They boldly told many others about Jesus.

The Holy Spirit comes to us today through Baptism, God's Word, and the Lord's Supper. The Spirit gives you a growing faith and helps you to live God's love every day. Hooray for the coming of the Holy Spirit!

We've got the Spirit!	*(Point thumbs to chest.)*
Yes, we do!	*(Make thumbs up sign.)*
God the Holy Spirit!	*(Place hands on heart.)*
How 'bout you?	*(Point to someone.)*

How do you show that the Holy Spirit lives in your heart? What do you do to show and tell that you believe in Jesus?

Cheer is from Son Times.
©1999 The Department of Child Ministry,
The Lutheran Church—Missouri Synod.
All rights reserved. Used by permission.

49

PART 3:
The Time of the
CHURCH

I n the first part of the church year, we paid great attention to major events in the life of Jesus. In this second part of the church year, we pay close attention to our own growth as His disciples. This is the "green season" of the year. It's all about growing stronger in our faith and love for Jesus and learning how to follow Him.

The Season after PENTECOST

Season after Pentecost
Color: Green

It's Not Easy Being Green

Season after Pentecost

"Go and make disciples of all nations, baptizing them in the name of the Father and of the Son and of the Holy Spirit, and teaching them to obey everything I have commanded you. And surely I am with you always, to the very end of the age" (Matthew 28:19–20).

The ***season after Pentecost*** celebrates the gift of the Holy Spirit. Through this gift, the church is able to tell about Jesus and do the ministry and mission He began. You hear the stories of the Holy Spirit at work in God's people helping His Church to grow.

Like the disciples, you wait for the Spirit to make the mission and ministry of Jesus your very own. At your Baptism, the power of the Holy Spirit begins to work in you. Your life is different. You act, speak, think, and listen in a new way. God's Church grows through you.

Pretend you are in the room with the disciples on the day of Pentecost. Draw a picture of yourself before and after the coming of the Holy Spirit. How did you change?

Before   After

First Sunday after PENTECOST

The First Sunday after Pentecost

Color: White

Three-in-One

The Holy Trinity

The Word became flesh and made His dwelling among us. We have seen His glory, the glory of the One and Only, who came from the Father, full of grace and truth (John 1:14).

We read in the Bible that God speaks of Himself as *three* Persons (Father, Son, and Holy Spirit), but only *one* God. That is why we refer to God as the Trinity, which means "three-in-one." Another word for "three-in-one" is triune. On **Holy Trinity**, you, along with the family of faith, celebrate all three Persons of your Triune God.

God is Father. Alleluia! *(Raise your left hand. God the Father is close to your heart.)*
God is Jesus. Alleluia! *(Raise your right hand. Jesus is God's "right-hand" man.)*
God is Spirit. Alleluia! *(Raise both hands and wiggle your fingers. The Spirit fans the flames of God's love to everyone.)*

The triangle often serves as the symbol, or design, that stands for the Trinity. Each side represents a Person of God. There are three sides, but one triangle. Other designs that stand for the Trinity are three circles linked together and a shamrock.

Create a *new* design that stands for the Trinity: God the Father, God the Son, and God the Holy Spirit.

REFORMATION DAY

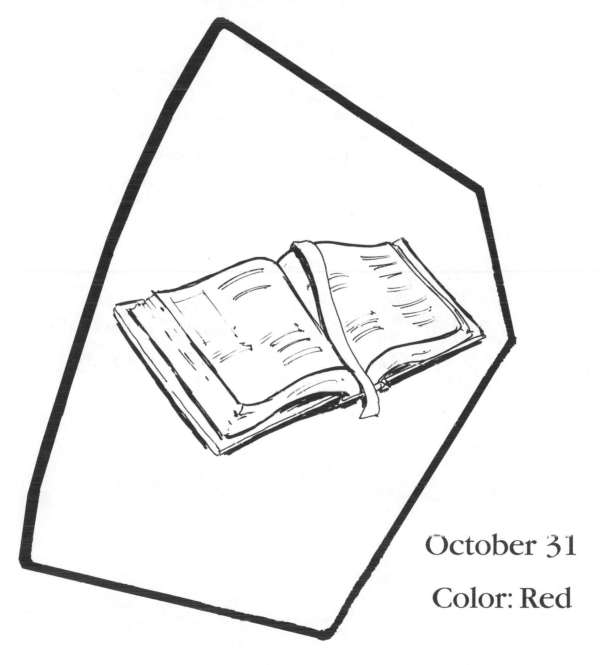

October 31

Color: Red

Reformation Day

October 31

"If you hold to My teaching, you are really My disciples. Then you will know the truth, and the truth will set you free" (John 8:31–32).

On **Reformation Day**, most Lutherans think about the man, Martin Luther. Martin Luther lived in the country of Germany. He spoke against some of the teachings of the church of that day which seemed to lead people away from Jesus and His love. Many people began to trust in themselves and their own good works, rather than in Jesus, their Savior.

The people who followed Martin Luther came to be known as Lutherans. Reformation Day is especially important for Lutherans because it points to the beginning of the Lutheran church. (Martin Luther, however, never liked the name Lutheran; he wanted people simply to be followers of Jesus.)

Martin Luther would probably tell you not to remember his life and work, but to use this day to remember Jesus. He would want you to know that because of Jesus:

* *God loves you freely.*
* *You can talk directly to God in prayer.*
* *You can be certain of life in heaven with God.*
* *You can live a courageous life for Jesus even when people are against you.*

56

ALL SAINTS' DAY

November 1
Color: Red

**A word picture of the gathering of all saints
in the Bible is found in Revelation 5:13.**

Now and Forever

All Saints' Day

"Rejoice and be glad, because great is your reward in heaven ..." (Matthew 5:12).

On **All Saints' Day** you remember saints of the church. Saints are special people to God and to His Church. They are forgiven sinners whom God has chosen to do His work in the world.

Some saints lived long before you and are now with God in heaven. Some saints are famous like St. Patrick, St. Valentine, and St. Nicholas. Everyone knows their names and sometimes their special days are celebrated all over the world.

Most saints are people like you. God forgives their sins and they go about their everyday lives doing God's work. They show and tell about Jesus in their homes, schools and churches, on the playground, and in grocery stores—wherever God has put them.

The church calls any sinner who is forgiven "saint." Are you a sinner? Are you forgiven? Does God use you to get His work done in the world? If so, then you can add your name to the saints of the church.

Write your first name using jumbo letters. Decorate each letter of your name.

One of the most important saints is *you!*

TakeNoteTogether

Enriching Activities for Kids and Their Grown-Ups

Now and Forever

All Saints' Day

All Saints' Day remembers not only those who died giving their lives for the sake of God but all people of God, living and dead, who form the entire family of faith in Christ. This day is observed on November 1 or the following Sunday.

 Plan an All Saints' party. Participants may want to dress up as saints who lived long ago.

 Get out old family photographs and together talk about relatives, past and present. Such conversations teach each generation about their heritage or the origins of their family.

 Tell stories about people who have helped to strengthen the faith of each of the baptized members of your household. A saint is a sinner who is forgiven. One doesn't need to have died to be numbered with the saints. Baptism makes each of us saints here and now.

 Pray for each person's baptismal godparents.

 Talk about teachers and pastors who have helped in your faith journey.

 Remember and give God thanks for friends and family members (especially those who have already gone to heaven) who set examples as faithful workers in the kingdom of God.

 Address each other as "Saint (individual's name)" for the day. Use this language without embarrassment (although it may get humorous).

There is something powerful to be taught here. This day in the Church's calendar helps us to remember who and what we are as baptized children of God! As you say "good night" on this day, remind one another of your Baptism and your resulting sainthood. God's work in you and your family is simply marvelous!

SUNDAY of the FULFILLMENT

**Last Sunday
of the Church Year
Color: Green**

Endings

Sunday of Fulfillment
or Christ the King Sunday

"Yes, I am coming soon." Amen. Come, Lord Jesus (Revelation 22:20).

People often have a party to celebrate when a big job is done. This Sunday, the **Sunday of the Fulfillment (Christ the King Sunday)**, is the Church's end-of-the-year party. The family of faith, having done the work of worship for a whole year, celebrates the awesome work of Jesus.

You often take gifts to parties, but in today's worship you remember that God is the great gift-giver, and the gift is Jesus. You thank God for another good year of worship. Worship is God giving the gift of Jesus to His people again and again. Jesus is the reason for the seasons of the church year.

On this day, the Sunday of Fulfillment, you celebrate that Jesus is King of kings and Lord of lords. You say thank You to Him with your prayers and praises. You sing songs that tell of His mighty work as Savior, and you remember His promise to come again. His coming will be more of a surprise than Christmas, or Palm Sunday, or even Easter, or Pentecost. You know King Jesus will come again. (You just don't know for sure when.)

St. Matthew, the writer of the first Gospel, often ends the stories about Jesus with these words: "This took place to fulfill what was said through the prophets." God kept (fulfilled) all of His promises in Jesus. So ... party!

Draw a crown as a party hat for an end-of-the-church-year party.

Beginnings

The Big Picture Puzzle

There is a time for everything, and a season for every activity under heaven (Ecclesiastes 3:1).

Each year the family of faith puts together a big puzzle. Each year the family of faith takes it apart and begins again in order to learn more about the pieces.

God's story is told every year. With the telling and retelling of each part of God's story, you come to understand His mighty acts of love, done for you! The end of the church year brings a new beginning. You will have another year to hear and share the good news about your powerful and loving God—seasons for celebrating His goodness.

Look at the stained glass window on the next page. Do you recognize the symbols of the church year? The entire church year fits together like a "Celebration Puzzle"—with Christ at the center.

You are also in God's story. The blank puzzle piece at the top of the window is for *your* picture. You are an important piece of the puzzle, but you are not the only piece. In this story you have an important job to do—adding more pieces to the puzzle.

God's story is for everyone.
God wants you to tell others about
His gift of Jesus. God's story never ends.
So, begin!